WHO BUILT THE FIRST HUMAN CIVILIZATION?

Ancient Mesopotamia
History Books for Kids
Children's Ancient History

BABY PROFESSOR
EDUCATION KIDS

Speedy Publishing LLC

40 E. Main St. #1156

Newark, DE 19711

www.speedypublishing.com

Copyright 2017

In this book, we're going to talk about the Sumerians in Ancient Mesopotamia. So, let's get right to it!

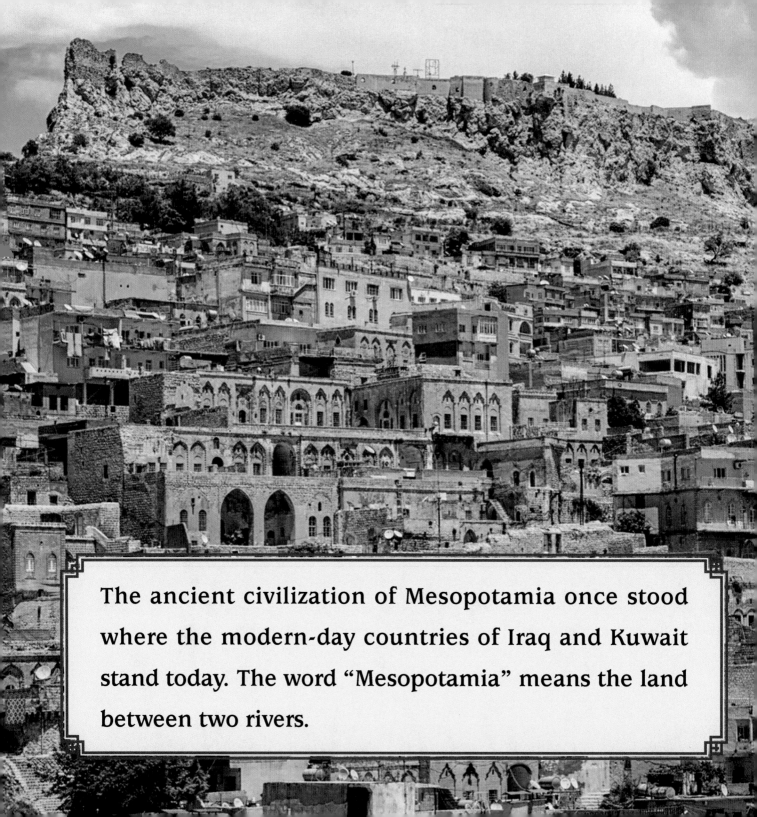

The ancient civilization of Mesopotamia once stood where the modern-day countries of Iraq and Kuwait stand today. The word "Mesopotamia" means the land between two rivers.

Mardin

Euphrates and Tigris

The rivers referred to were the Tigris and Euphrates. Between these two water sources there were fertile lands where the first civilization began.

THE CRADLE OF CIVILIZATION

Sumer was located in the southern portion of Mesopotamia. It has been labeled the "cradle of civilization." The word "Sumer" comes from the Akkadian language, which was used in the northern part of Mesopotamia, and it translates to "the land where the kings are civilized."

Ur

The Sumerians simply called their people "the black-headed people." When they referred to their own country, they called it "the land" or "the land where the black-headed people live."

Sumer is mentioned in the Book of Genesis in the Bible and there it is called Shinar. The Sumerians believed that the gods gave the first human society the gifts that were needed to build a civilization. These gods founded Eridu, a city in the Sumer region. Although archaeologists believe that Uruk was the oldest city ever established, the ancient people of Mesopotamia believed that all civilization sprang from Eridu.

The Ruins of Eridu

Ur

THE UBAID PERIOD

Archaeologists, historians, and scientists have long debated when civilization began. It was thought that Sumer was settled around 4500 BC. However, there's now evidence that human activity took place there even earlier.

The Sumerians were not the first people there. Prior to them there was a group now called the Ubaid people, named after the mound of al-Ubaid where their artifacts were discovered. They are sometimes called Proto-Euphrateans, which simply designates that they were some of the earliest people to live in the area of the Euphrates River.

Euphrates River

Ubaid Period Pottery

Not much is known about the Ubaid people, but their artifacts prove that they were no longer hunters and gatherers. They were already cultivating food to feed themselves. Hoes for tilling the soil, knives for cutting stalks, and sickles for chopping down crops were found among their artifacts. They also created figurines as well as painted pottery. It's not known when the Sumerians came into the region where the Ubaid people were living.

THE SUMERIAN KING LIST

The Sumerians made a record of all their kings on a huge stone tablet written over 4,000 years ago in their language of cuneiform. The list was prepared by a scribe from Lagash, one of the major cities of Sumer. Copies of this list in various forms have been found on more than one artifact and it is a mysterious document.

Sumerian Clay Tablet

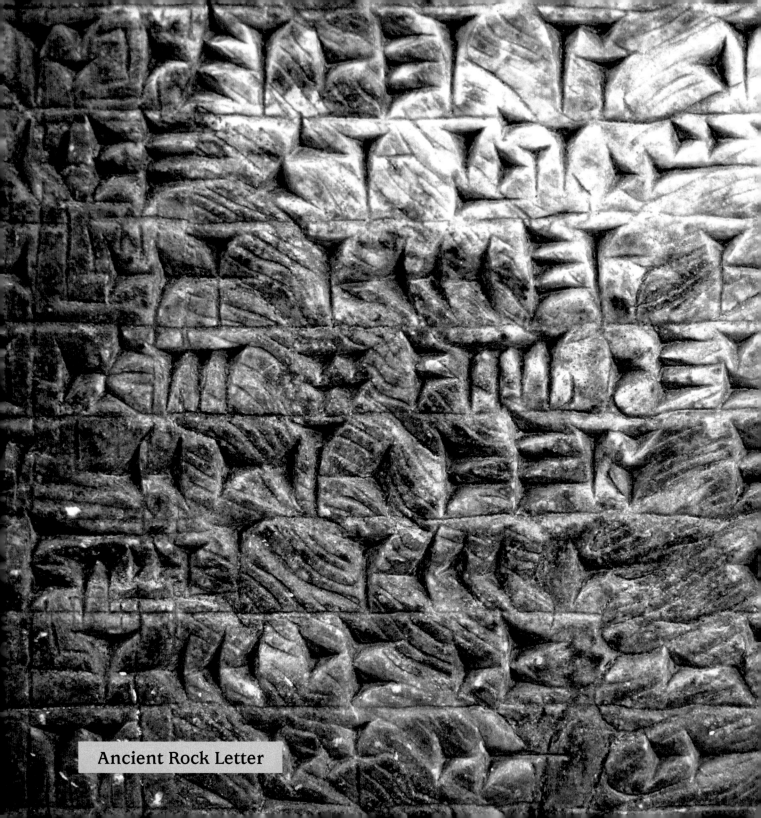

Ancient Rock Letter

Archaeologists and historians are somewhat at a loss as to how to interpret it. The reason is that the beginning kings mentioned are supposedly gods who reigned for many thousands of years.

The Sumerians believed that this document showed how their kings were directly connected to the earlier gods who ruled. The "Great Flood" is mentioned in the list, just as it is in the Bible. After that, men ruled and the first such king is a king called Etana of Kish.

Sumerian Statue

Clay Tablet

It's believed that the King List was put together to show that civilization happened after the gods showed men how to create order from chaos. Some historians believe that when the list was put together around 2100 BC, it had a specific mission. Its mission was to show that the king who was called Utu-Hegal from Uruk was of royal lineage that went all the way back to the times of the gods.

Many of the kings listed were either gods, demigods, or superheroes so it is difficult to know how many of the Sumerians' descriptions were factual. Etana of Kish was famous for going up to heaven on an eagle's back. King Dumuzi the Shepherd and King Gilgamesh are both described in epic poems as heroes having superhuman qualities.

The Statue of Gilgamesh

Kubaba

The King List includes the name of a woman ruler as well. She was called Kubaba and is listed as the keeper of a tavern who took the throne around 2500 BC. According to the list she "reinforced the foundations of Kish" and created a dynasty that lasted for one century after her reign.

The Sumerians believed that all human activity had been set in motion through the gods. The job of their rulers and all humans was to maintain order and keep chaos at bay. The early Sumerian writers concentrated on the gods and these legends in their ancient writings so their stone tablets don't give archaeologists and historians that many clues about their day-to-day lives. All of those details have come from other artifacts.

Sumerian Tablet

Sumerians

THE RISE OF CITIES

By 3600 BC, the Sumerians had invented a tremendous amount of technology they could use to create order from chaos. They had created the wheel, the first vehicles that had wheels, cuneiform writing, which had evolved from earlier pictograms, the first sailboats, some of the first farming processes including systems of irrigation, a form of government, and the idea of city planning.

Their number system used the number 60 as its base. They devised the idea of 60 minutes within an hour as well as the idea of 360 degrees within a circle. Although 10 is the base of our modern number system, we still use these ideas within our measurement of time and geometry today.

Ruins of a Ziggurat at the Sumerian City of Kish

They observed the movements of the moon and stars and used their observations to create a working calendar. All of their innovations were passed on to subsequent civilizations.

Historians believe that writing was invented so that the Sumerians could communicate at distances as they traded with other regions. Ancient scribes were well versed with hundreds of cuneiform wedge-shaped characters. They wrote their words and syllables on clay tablets that were still wet using a stylus made from a reed. After the writing was complete, the tablet was placed out in the sun to dry and harden.

Cuneiform Tablet

Although their writing was first used for the everyday accounting needs and the recording of business matters, over the centuries it was used for literature, poetry, history, and codes of law. There is evidence that it was in use for over 3,000 years and was adopted by more than ten varying cultures.

Archaeologists have found that astronomy texts from the Near East were written using cuneiform characters all the way up to the first century AD, many centuries after the Sumerian civilization was long gone.

Tablet with Cuneiform Inscription

Kingdom of Lagash Ruins

Although the countries of China and India profess to have had the world's first cities, most historians accept that Sumer was the site of the very first cities, with Uruk as the world's first city. Some of these cities, such as Eridu, Ur, Isin, and Lagash may have been founded as villages as early as 5000 BC. Uruk was the largest as well as the most influential during its peak. To build their structures, the Sumerians used bricks that they created from clay that were dried in the sun.

SUMERIAN CITY-STATES

As the civilization of Sumer grew larger and the cities gained in population, they created city-states. The ruling body or government of a city-state would rule the urban area as well as the farmland that surrounded it. Just as in the later Greek civilization, these city-states would often be at war with each other.

Interior of an Assyrian Palace

Ziggarut of Ur

When this happened, the people living outside the city would run to behind the city's walls for safety. It's believed that some of the city-states became very populated. It's estimated that the city-state called Ur might have had as many as 65,000 inhabitants at its height.

There were many city-states, such as Sippar, Bad-tibura, and Shuruppak, and each one had its own ruler who had the title of Lugal or Ensi. These rulers were like kings who had their own kingdom or governors reigning over a province. To give them even more power, they were usually the high priests of the Sumerian religion also.

Sumerian Worshipper

The kings were not the only government officials. The system of government was formed with a network of officials who were in charge of the city's construction projects and who kept the city running

Restored Ziggurat in Ancient Ur

smoothly. They had laws to maintain order as well. Citizens were expected to follow the established laws or face punishment for their disobedience.

RELIGION

In addition to having its own ruler, each city-state had a god of its own. The city center had a very large ziggurat. The ziggurat was a temple that was designed as a pyramid with stepped-up sides. Its top was flat.

Ziggurat

The Tower of Babel

At the Ziggurat, the high priest would offer sacrifices and perform ceremonies and rituals in honor of the city's god. There's some evidence that the ziggurat at Eridu may have been the Tower of Babel that's discussed in the Holy Bible.

Awesome! Now you know more about the first human civilization in Sumer in Ancient Mesopotamia. You can find more Ancient History books from Baby Professor by searching the website of your favorite book retailer.

Made in the USA
Monee, IL
29 June 2023